Vision

Found in 1 Js

   - Ebook

No vision and you perish;

No Ideal, and you're lost;

Your heart must ever cherish

Some faith at any cost.

Some hope, some dream to cling to,

Some rainbow in the sky,

Some melody to sing to,

Some service that is high.

—HARRIET DU AUTERMONT

VISION

AWAKENING YOUR POTENTIAL TO
CREATE A BETTER WORLD

Peter L. Benson

TEMPLETON PRESS

Templeton Press
300 Conshohocken State Road, Suite 550
West Conshohocken, PA 19428
www.templetonpress.org

Typeset and designed by Gopa and Ted2, Inc.

Library of Congress Cataloging-in-Publication Data

Benson, Peter L.
Vision : awakening your potential to create
a better world / Peter L. Benson.
p. cm.
ISBN-13: 978-1-59947-248-5 (pbk. : alk. paper)
ISBN-10: 1-59947-248-1 (pbk. : alk. paper)
1. Self-actualization (Psychology). 2. Social action.
I. Title.
BF637.S4B464 2009
158—dc22
2008040962

Printed in the United States of America

09   10   11   12   13   14   10 9 8 7 6 5 4 3 2 1

For James Dittes, Bernard Spilka,

and Merton Strommen—

beacons on the path

CONTENTS

VISION

Another world is not only possible,

she is on her way. On a quiet day,

I can hear her breathing.

**—ARUNDHATI ROY, INDIAN AUTHOR
AND PEACE ACTIVIST**

1. VISION

....

vision: vizh en (n) **1:** the act or power of imagination **2:** the act or power of seeing **3:** unusual discernment or foresight **4:** an imaginative conception of the future

....

THE CAPACITY to generate vision is among life's most beautiful and unheralded gifts. As the definitions above reveal, it is a powerful act—this art of seeing and articulating what's possible. As with other human capabilities, however, too often we fail to recognize this power. And too rarely do we engage in vision-making, much less make a commitment to realizing our vision.

Many of us don't take the time, first of all, to inhabit visionary space, to discern and honor our inner promptings and passions. Regrettably, many of us also believe that vision-making is a province reserved for a select few. Regarding George Bernard Shaw's famous saying, "You see things and you say, 'Why?' But I dream things that never were and say 'Why not?,'" some are apt to assume that the words apply only to him and other renowned dreamers, not to themselves.

Others equate a vision with a goal. Our diverse goals—to lose weight, to sail the Aegean, to earn a certain salary—may involve *envisioning* a desired end, but vision goes far beyond mere goals. Goals, of course, encourage us to improve and enrich our lives. They give us a sense of control, order, and direction. From month to month and from year to year, however, they are likely to change. If you're like me, you may revisit a few of them on New Year's Eve and lament how little progress you made toward reaching them over the course of the previous year.

Vision: Inspired and Inspiring

Vision, on the other hand, is of another order entirely. It's inspired and it inspires. That is, we sense that the conception is rooted in something greater than ourselves or our individual concerns, something enduring. It often encompasses a big truth, a higher purpose. It pulls us toward the future.

Vision is a summons. Values come into play when we imagine what can be. Accordingly, the result is also an image of what *should* be. Any vision, at its best, excites people to join hands in advancing the greater good.

Consider one example of vision-at-its-best: the Declaration of Independence, a document that helped to birth a nation grounded in "certain unalienable rights . . . among these . . . life, liberty and the pursuit of happiness."

So many of our dreams at first seem impossible,

then they seem improbable, and then,

when we summon the will,

they soon become inevitable.

**—CHRISTOPHER REEVE,
AMERICAN ACTOR AND ACTIVIST**

And recall the words of the American visionary, Martin Luther King Jr., whose word-pictures in his memorable "I Have a Dream" speech, described what, with shared vision and will, could and should be.

King expressed a dream that descendants of former slaves and former slave owners would be able to sit down together, creating a new community. He shared his vision that his own four little children would one day live in a nation "where they will not be judged by the color of their skin but by the content of their character." And he invoked a biblical vision, adopted as his own:

> I have a dream that one day every valley shall be exalted, every hill and mountain shall be made low, the rough places will be made plain, and the crooked places will be made straight, and the glory of the Lord shall be revealed, and all flesh shall see it together.

If I were to wish for anything, I should not wish for
wealth and power, but for the passionate sense of
the potential, for the eye which, ever young and
ardent, sees the possible. Pleasure disappoints,
possibility never. And what wine is
so sparkling, what so fragrant, what
so intoxicating, as possibility!

—SØREN KIERKEGAARD,
DANISH PHILOSOPHER

. . . . .

Hope is a waking dream.

—ARISTOTLE

It was nearly two hundred years after the framing of the Declaration that King dramatically and poignantly reminded Americans of the most central value in the vision of the nation's founders: "We hold these truths to be self-evident—that all men are created equal." King was still holding fast to the dream, even while it remained for many a promise unfulfilled, as he stood on the steps of the Lincoln Memorial. He said, "I have a dream that one day this nation will rise up and live out the meaning of its creed."

Encompassing the "Big Picture"

The thread that extends from the Declaration of Independence to King's 1963 speech, and beyond, is a symbolic one. The enduring existence of these threads, whether they extend from one community to another or from one generation to another, are characteristic of the way vision plays out in history—personal or public. It is the nature of vision to encompass the "big picture." Implicit in a vision is the understanding that it may well take a long time to achieve what is imagined, if indeed the vision is ever fully achievable.

The election of Barack Obama as the forty-fourth president represents both vision achieved and vision renewed. On the one hand, we see America rising above race to choose a man based on his merits, on character. When we listen carefully, however, to Obama's message, as articulated during his acceptance speech at the Democratic National Convention on August 28, 2008, he says that the idea of a just society for all still awaits us. The American promise—of prosperity and opportunity for each and all—is the shared vision that still "binds us together in spite of our differences, that makes us fix our eye not on what is seen, but what is unseen; that better place around the bend."

Forging a Common Purpose

Vision-at-its-best captivates and energizes people. The vision and the en-visioner inspire a collective enterprise. One by one, each "owns" the vision, personally. Together, all join hands in repairing one or another aspect of a broken world.

Thus, two key characteristics of vision are that, first, it is usually long term and "big picture" and, second, realizing it requires many hearts and souls, committed to a shared and common purpose.

Recognizing Our Interdependence

There is a subtle—and I think critical—idea implicit in the sustained pursuit of an inspired vision that relates to *interdependence*. The framers of the Declaration clearly recognized its importance, that my right to pursue

Give to us clear vision that we may know where to stand and what to stand for—because unless we stand for something, we shall fall for anything.

—PETER MARSHALL, U.S. SENATE CHAPLAIN

.....

The failure to read good books both enfeebles the vision and strengthens our most fatal tendency—the belief that the here and now is all there is.

—ALLAN BLOOM, AMERICAN PHILOSOPHER

happiness is inextricably intertwined with yours.

Perhaps the silver lining in the current global environmental crisis is the reiteration or rediscovery of this essential truth: All of life exists as an organic web of connectedness. My carbon footprint impacts your life and your children's, and yours has the same effect on mine. Creation of a carbon-neutral world calls for all hands on deck. If we are to preserve the planet and life as we know it, each of us—not just a few of us—has to find the vision compelling enough to act on it, and to act in concert with the global community.

One Example: My Nonprofit

The nonprofit organization I lead, Search Institute, involves this kind of long-term, "big picture" vision and great interdependence among those who commit to it. We use the tools of social science research, publishing, and training to mobilize and equip citizens and communities to "grow great kids."

Creating "a world where all young people are valued and thrive"—the core of our vision statement—may seem like an overwhelming or hopelessly idealistic dream. Just think about the scope of the problems of youth—both domestically and internationally—the complexity of changing public policy, and the massive number of economic, political, and social issues that come into play. Considering all these issues, the challenge of realizing this vision seems daunting, the vision itself almost ridiculously audacious.

It's our mission statement that provides our rallying cry—to "provide leadership, knowledge and practical resources to promote healthy children, youth and communities." Here's the reminder of the concrete steps we take day in and day out to keep the dream alive and to bring it closer to fruition, as hundreds of communities across America join with us to realize the ultimate vision. We focus on what is immediately before us—making a contribution—and hold fast to the dream.

As we envision the change we seek, we anticipate how that change will play out in the real world. This anticipatory hope inspires continued action. Our mission gives us the impetus to be faithful to the vision and reminds us of how we are making a contribution, along with many others around the world, all of whom are dedicated to growing great kids.

The audacious dream becomes do-able as we acknowledge all the other persons and organizations on the planet working toward permutations of this vision in the interest of children's well-being. We are better when they are better. They nurture us, inspire us. We inspire and nurture them. Spiritually speaking, countless interdependent others simultaneously move toward the light of a

We are approaching a new age of synthesis.
Knowledge cannot be merely a degree or a skill . . .
it demands a broader vision, capabilities in critical
thinking and logical deduction without which
we cannot have constructive progress.

—LI KA-SHING, CHINESE MULTIBILLIONAIRE
ENTREPRENEUR

. . . . .

Vision is perhaps our greatest strength . . .
it has kept us alive to the power and continuity
of thought through the centuries, it makes
us peer into the future and lends shape
to the unknown.

—LI KA-SHING

new day for *all* children and young people everywhere.

VISION-AT-ITS-BEST: GROUNDED IN OUR SEARCH FOR MEANING

Vision-at-its-best calls forth the celebration of interdependence, whether these visions relate to preservation of the natural world, world peace, thriving youth, or innumerable other exhilarating ends, requiring all kinds of cooperation and collaboration.

It is in our nature to see and imagine what can be. Helen Keller wrote: "The most pathetic person in the world is someone who has sight, but has no vision." Keller makes it clear that we do not have to be visionaries like Thomas Jefferson, John Adams, or Martin Luther King Jr. Her words suggest that each and every one of us can lay claim to a visionary calling.

It is difficult to say what is impossible, for the
dream of yesterday is the hope of today
and the reality of tomorrow.

**—ROBERT H. GODDARD, AMERICAN PHYSICIST
AND ROCKETRY EXPERT**

. . . . .

I dwell in Possibility—

A fairer House than Prose—

**—EMILY DICKINSON,
AMERICAN POET**

Whether vision rises up out of our own life experiences and dreams or comes to us via another's bold example, which we feel inspired to adopt as our own, it is the spark that links us to what is meaningful about living in this world. Embracing a vision is a corollary to making a contribution. It follows from our innate search for meaning. It is in our nature to imagine what is possible.

I live not in dreams but in contemplation of

a reality that is perhaps the future.

**—RAINER MARIA RILKE, AUSTRIAN POET
AND NOVELIST**

.....

To accomplish great things,

we must dream as well as act.

**—ANATOLE FRANCE,
FRENCH NOVELIST**

2. VISIONARY

visionary (n.) **1:** a person with unusual foresight **2:** having or marked by foresight and imagination

THE FIRST living, breathing visionary to introduce me to "possibility thinking" was Albert Schweitzer. Growing up outside of Chicago, in Joliet, Illinois, I became conscious of the work that followed from his vision. Because a teacher exposed me to his story, at the age of twelve or thirteen, I learned of Dr. Schweitzer's commitment to people in equatorial Africa. It left a deep impression.

One aspect of Dr. Schweitzer's life that animated my thinking was his choice to go against the prevailing theological mood of his time. He professed a conviction that the measure of faith is living a life of compassion. The purpose of life, he said, was to serve. He stood out for me as a person who acted from the courage of his convictions. And this twist on faith both compelled and propelled him to live a life he might not have imagined at an early age—as he helped and healed countless fellow humans with whatever means were available to him.

HONORING A VISION

This model of honoring a vision broke into my life at a formative time. Dr. Schweitzer's example offered testament to the energizing power of living as a change agent in the world. He set the bar very high. Nevertheless, he enlisted many recruits to follow in his footsteps as healers and helpers. His story infused me with energy and the impetus to imagine a life enriched by vision as well.

J. K. Rowling, who has written seven novels in the *Harry Potter* series, selling, at this writing, more than 400 million copies, admits that the idea of Harry Potter "came [to her] fully formed," characters and situations flooding into her head one day during a cross-country train trip. Despite numerous obstacles in her path, she honored the vision and wrote. She says, "I wrote the story I meant to write." That is, she held fast to her vision, knowing that she risked losing readers along the way. She and her characters would not "be deflected, either by adoration or by criticism."

In a powerful commencement address at Harvard in June 2008, she revealed that she has possessed since childhood what her parents called an "overactive imagination." They were convinced that these imaginings

We are the music makers, and we are
the dreamers of dreams.

—ARTHUR O'SHAUGHNESSY,
BRITISH POET

would never translate into meaningful work. But Rowling learned to trust in her imagination, to believe in its power, and to let it guide her life. She was born, she knew, to write stories. This visionary is now the highest-earning novelist in history, but, more important, acting on her vision ultimately launched a new generation of readers, adults among them, worldwide.

"Imagination," she told the graduating seniors, "is not only the uniquely human capacity to envision that which is not," but it is "the fount of all invention and innovation."

Albert Einstein expressed a similar conviction when he asserted that "imagination is more important than knowledge."

VISIONARIES IN MY LIFE

I'm aware that from the second decade of my life to the present, models and mentors whom I now recognize as "visionaries" entered my life and helped to shape it. It is not as if I was bent on finding them. Rather, it's as though they sought me out.

A few who come to mind include Martin Luther King Jr., whose social vision influenced my thinking in high school and college. During graduate school, I became aware of the visionary stance of both William Sloane Coffin, the iconoclastic chaplain and peace activist at Yale, and Reinhold Niebuhr, the social philosopher and theologian. Over the next twenty years, the movers and shakers whose visions exhilarated and motivated me most often imagined a safer, more just, and more sustainable world.

Recently, I find myself adding another kind of prophetic voice to the list of inspirational leaders guiding my life—visionaries speaking to the interior life, explorers of inner space. Luminaries like William James, Carl Jung, and Joseph Campbell were among my guides. And to the "old guard" I've now been adding still other visionaries, like the Dalai Lama and Eckhart Tolle, to the list.

STRENGTHENING COLLECTIVE CONSCIOUSNESS

In so doing, I feel a part of some cosmic continuity, a collective consciousness that nudges humankind toward balance and integration. This awareness lifts me up as it challenges me to play a part.

I learn something about myself by ruminating on how these mentors and models have influenced my own decisions and actions, whether their role has been to reaffirm the possibility of social justice—the obligation to engage locally and globally—or to deepen my metaphysical discernment.

Like dream analysis, this "vision analysis" prompts a look at our deeper selves and what

A vision is just not a picture of what could be:

it is an appeal to our better selves,

a call to become something more.

**—ROSABETH MOSS KANTER, AUTHOR AND HARVARD
BUSINESS PROFESSOR**

. . . . .

Imagination is more important

than knowledge. Knowledge is limited.

Imagination encircles the world.

—ALBERT EINSTEIN

we are becoming. It's illuminating to discover the visionaries who first come to mind when deciding which ones speak to you.

Anyone's list will, of course, be arbitrary and distinctive. There are biases built in to any short list, since the beauty and value of a vision is, invariably, in the eye of the beholder. Nevertheless, I'll offer a few representative names across a broad spectrum of endeavors, hoping to awaken in you thoughts of other inspirational figures who have influenced your own path in life.

VISIONARIES IN DIVERSE FIELDS

This admittedly incomplete and spontaneously created taxonomy would surely include artistic visionaries like Pablo Picasso, Frank Lloyd Wright, R. Buckminster Fuller, Helen Frankenthaler, and Georgia O'Keeffe. Inspirational models of honoring and preserving the natural world include Rachel Carson,

If you can imagine it, you can achieve it.

If you can dream it, you can become it.

—WILLIAM ARTHUR WARD,
AMERICAN AUTHOR

. . . . .

Hope is a waking dream.

—ARISTOTLE,
GREEK PHILOSOPHER

Jane Goodall, and Al Gore. Bill and Melinda Gates as well as Sir John Marks Templeton are examples of a growing number of philanthropic visionaries.

Perhaps one of these social visionaries—Susan B. Anthony, Sojourner Truth, Jane Addams, Mahatma Gandhi, Che Guevera, Gloria Steinem, or Nelson Mandela—would be on your list of world changers, dreamers. Leaders in the business world and in the province of science and technology might include Thomas Edison, Henry Ford, Walt Disney, Steve Jobs, William Hewlett, and David Packard. Perhaps Virginia Wolff comes to mind as a literary visionary whose writing has influenced you; Aldous Huxley or H. G. Wells could as readily be the writers whose work shaped your thinking. How about in the arena of music? Bob Dylan, Quincy Jones, and Thelonius Monk come to my mind. Ludwig von Beethoven, Johann Sebastian Bach, and Wolfgang Amadeus Mozart might

For me, the child is a veritable image of becoming,
of possibility, poised to reach towards what is
not yet, towards a growing that cannot be
predetermined or prescribed. I see her and
I fill the space with others like her, risking,
straining, wanting to find out, to ask
their own questions, to experience
a world that is shared.

**—MAXINE GREENE, AMERICAN PHILOSOPHER
AND EDUCATOR**

hold premier spots as musical visionaries for you. Spiritual visionaries may rate a place on your list—whether they be Kathleen Raine, Hildegard of Bingen, Matthew Fox, Richard Bucke, Thomas Merton, Deepak Chopra, Ralph Waldo Emerson, or Desmond Tutu.

The challenge is to take a trip through time, from childhood or adolescence to the present moment, to ponder whose visions have already influenced your own or which visionaries inspire you to generate your own vision of what can be. In other words, consider the following questions:

- Who inspired you when you were a teenager? Why?
- Who are the visionaries who inspire you now? Why?
- Do you see similarities among those who inspire you? Over time, has the field of or your focus on influential visionaries shifted?

- Across your whole life, whose vision has most awakened or changed you?

The process begs to be shared with family and friends, making for engaging dialogue with your partner, your children, or your colleagues. The choices provide illuminating insights related to which visions have the power to motivate and mobilize each person.

TAKING RISKS TO REALIZE A VISION

A vision can be so captivating, so compelling, that individuals are willing to regularly put themselves in harm's way to achieve an end guided by their vision. We are all aware of visionaries whose work has been a threat to the status quo, whose perspective has incited a violent reaction.

Commitment to the "big picture" can be risky business. I think immediately of the assassinations of John F. Kennedy, Robert Kennedy, and Martin Luther King Jr. Perhaps you know or have known someone who has put his life in danger in order to honor a vision.

One dear friend of mine, Bill Sampson, shared a vision with others to reveal and challenge the dreadful working conditions faced by a predominantly African American workforce in the textile mills of North Carolina. Bill worked side by side with the mill workers to document firsthand the despicable work environment. He and his compatriots talked to laborers about unionizing as a way to finally address safety violations, health hazards, substandard pay, and other unfair labor practices, which had been the norm for decades.

The man, who as a young boy had come upon a cross burned on a neighbor's lawn and vowed then and there to one day combat such hatred and injustice, took a bullet

If you can dream it, you can do it.

—WALT DISNEY,
AMERICAN ANIMATOR

to his head during a demonstration demanding workers' rights. While local Greensboro authorities looked on, sharpshooters—whom evidence suggests were members of the Ku Klux Klan—murdered Bill and a number of his fellow activists on that sunny afternoon.

Children Embracing Their Visions

A twelve-year-old boy—Iqbal Masih, born in Islamabad, Pakistan—claimed a vision of a better world, based on his own grueling personal experience. Sold into slavery at the age of four by his parents for $16, Iqbal spent six years shackled to a carpet-weaving loom as he tied small knots into the rugs, hour after hour, day after day. Freed of this yoke, at last, at the age of twelve, Iqbal envisioned an international crusade to end child labor.

Just as the world began to listen, an assassin shot and killed the boy as he was riding his bicycle in the Pakistani village of Muridke in 1995. It was widely hinted that members of the carpet industry, angered and threatened by the growing international outrage over a system that exploits children, were responsible for silencing the voice of the child who had dared to challenge that system.

Iqbal remains an exemplar of a magnificent corps of visionary youth. I am fortunate to witness such young visionaries in action, particularly at the Search Institute annual conference called Healthy Communities • Healthy Youth, which draws up to two thousand adults and young people each year from all fifty states and a number of other countries. Here, adults and youth learn from each other how to transform communities and provide kids with what they need to succeed. At each conference, the most spellbinding keynote speeches invariably come from young people, passionate about their dreams for changing the world.

Craig Kielburger, half a world away from

Iqbal Masih's birthplace, was one of them. One day, Craig, who grew up in a comfortable, middle-class family in Ontario, Canada, was hunched over his cereal bowl and about to scan the newspaper for his favorite comic strip, when his gaze fell on this front-page headline:

Battled Child Labour, Boy, 12, Murdered

It was in that defining moment, that Craig, also twelve years old, caught the vision bug. He began reading about Iqbal Masih, child labor, and slavery, ultimately asking his teacher for permission to speak about the subject to his fellow seventh-graders. He related what he knew about Iqbal's story and that of other child laborers, then asked, "Does anyone want to help me fight for children's rights?"

Eleven hands shot up, and Free the Children was born—an organization originally

I don't know what the future may hold,
but I know who holds the future.

**—RALPH ABERNATHY,
AMERICAN CIVIL RIGHTS ACTIVIST**

.....

The way to live our vision on a daily basis
is to understand that right now is the
only time we have.

**—JOHN HANLEY,
LEADERSHIP GURU**

with no infrastructure or business plan—only kids writing petitions, giving speeches, holding garage sales to raise funds, persuading adults to come on board, starting chapters in other schools. Ten years later, in 2005, Free the Children became the world's largest international network of children mobilized to advocate for education, health care, and children's rights.

One million children in North America alone call themselves members. Here is a compelling vision, "inspiring young people as socially conscious global citizens to become agents of change for their peers around the world." Needless to say, Craig's presentation at the Healthy Communities • Healthy Youth podium was mesmerizing, even galvanizing, winning hundreds of new converts from the ranks of conference participants.

Idealism Dovetailing with the
Search for Identity

The search for identity at this stage of development, combined with a passionate idealism and a readiness to make a difference, make such appeals difficult to ignore. An electric current moved through the crowd of youth, as they imagined their part in such a cause.

Another exhilarating keynote came one year from Erin Gruwell, whose work as a young, inexperienced, but visionary teacher had a transformative effect on the lowest-performing students at Woodrow Wilson High School in Long Beach, California. She and her students wrote a book about their journey together, titled *The Freedom Writers' Diary: How a Teacher and 150 Teens Used Writing to Change Themselves and the World Around Them,* which has inspired educators and teens around the globe. (The book was also made into a major motion picture, called *Freedom Writers*.)

Erin refused to adopt the defeatist attitude of certain educators and most of the kids around her; her vision included awakening these so-called throwaway kids to their enormous potential and purpose. In the process of inspiring them to tell their individual authentic stories in written form, she transformed a classroom culture of anger, violence, and hopelessness into one of anticipation of what could be.

In their own words, they told their stories and invited the world to see youth—all youth—through a different lens, enlisting others in schools and communities around the world to help kids thrive. This continues to be the message Erin Gruwell, now president of the Freedom Writers Foundation, propounds whenever she speaks. It's a message to which I naturally relate, as did the young people at the conference when Erin

spoke. They lined up for hundreds of auto-
graphed copies of the book.

ADOLESCENCE: WHEN VISION
OFTEN TAKES HOLD

A person's lifelong attraction to the power
of vision often begins in adolescence. This is
true of my own story as well. And it is con-
firmed in the academic study of adolescence.
Idealism springs forth in spades from ages
thirteen to twenty-one. It's nature's way of
birthing a new generation of visionaries. We
ought to be thankful for that. As Desmond
Tutu noted, "Youth are uniquely equipped
to change the world . . . they choose not to
accept what is, but to imagine what might
be." However, many parents and teachers
(and adults in general) are driven crazy by
the way young visionaries challenge them to
walk the talk. In my life, I want to give wings
to visionary neophytes. They will be, as J. K.

Rowling put it, the "mothers and fathers" of invention and innovation.

Of course, in the words of George Eliot, "It is never too late to be what you might have been." By celebrating the visionary exuberance of youth, I do not mean to suggest that vision-making and inspired action are exclusively the province of the young. I share the view of the novelist Gabriel Garcia Márquez who wrote:

It is not true that people stop pursuing dreams because they grow old.

They grow old because they stop pursuing dreams.

Deep in the human heart

The fire of justice burns;

A vision of a world renewed

Through radical concern.

**—WILLIAM L. WALLACE,
NEW ZEALAND HYMN-WRITER**

3. VISION &
THE SOCIAL GOOD

....

THE VISIONS that inspire you and me are often directed to improving the lives of people. The focus can range from a local community to a nation or to the entire world. The idea of the necessity and importance of vision has been around for a long, long time.

VISION IN THE BIBLE

More than 2,500 years ago, Old Testament scribes created a canon of human wisdom that many of us know as the Book of Proverbs.

Chapter 29 contains a number of admonitions directed at parents as they work to forge their children's character. For our purposes, here's the central one: "Where there is no vision, the people perish" (Proverbs 29:18). This saying has become widely adopted in contemporary culture. It is a favorite of politicians and social reformers. It is probably on a bumper sticker somewhere. And it's taken completely out of context.

Biblical scholars say that, at its core, this verse has to do with listening to and following the Word of God. The Word of God was the ultimate authority, so the central idea here is we had better unite around the rule of God or we will not survive. This becomes more obvious when we read the second part of the verse. In its entirety, Proverbs 29:18 goes like this: "Where there is no vision, the people perish; but he that keepeth the law, happy is he."

It also makes a difference which biblical

translation we consult. Here are a couple of telling variations:

- Without prophetic vision people run wild, but blessed are those who follow God's teachings.

- Where there is no revelation, the people cast off restraint; but one who keeps the law is blessed.

I am no expert on biblical exegesis, but what is interesting to me is that the original intent of the proverb seems to be about exerting social control. It is God's revealed will that provides the framework for how to live—and how to survive in a hostile world. Now, in the popular usage of the verse, it is viewed as compelling us to bring about social change. I'm all for that, even if we are taking the quote out of context.

Franklin Delano Roosevelt became our thirty-second president during one of our

Don't believe all of the negative perceptions that
are out there about youth. You, along with your
families and communities, can change things.
You need to be part of a network of peers and
adults who can work together to achieve a
vision you may have . . . Young people are
not in a "waiting period" . . . waiting to be
leaders, waiting to make a difference . . .
young people matter now!

—BARBARA TAVERAS,
AMERICAN PHILANTHROPIST

nation's stormiest periods—the Great Depression. Wages had declined 60 percent in value; more than 25 percent of wage earners were out of work. Hundreds of thousands of people lost their life savings, their homes, their businesses. If there was ever a time for big vision, it was then. Hope that things would get better was critically needed, or escalating despair could have easily crippled the American experiment, and left our economy in shambles for decades to come.

FDR: A Vision of the Common Good

It is March 4, 1933. FDR walks to the podium to deliver his inaugural address to Congress and the American people. Early in the speech, he utters these famous words: "So, first of all, let me assert my firm belief that the only thing we have to fear is fear itself—nameless, unreasoning, unjustified terror which paralyzes needed efforts to convert retreat into advance." The president then goes on to explain how our nation got into this mess. The "evildoers" are the money people: "The rulers of the exchange of mankind's goods have failed, through their own stubbornness and their own incompetence. The practices of the unscrupulous money changers stand indicted in the court of public opinion, rejected by the hearts and minds of men."

And why are the money changers so derelict, so selfish, so destructive? Because they care about themselves rather than the larger social collective. Here's the proof text: "They only know the rules of a generation of self-seekers. *They have no vision, and when there is no vision, the people perish*" (emphasis added).

Roosevelt then calls on the American people to put aside self-interest and commit to a common and unifying vision. The rallying cry goes like this: "If I read the temper of our people correctly, we now realize, as we have never realized before, our interdependence on each other; that we cannot merely take but we must give as well; that if we are to go forward, we must move as a trained and loyal army willing to sacrifice for the good of a common discipline." The commander-in-chief, we see, is mobilizing the troops to implement his vision of a better society.

JFK: A Vision Looking Skyward

Thirty years later—in a much different time—John F. Kennedy also invokes Proverbs 29:18. The mood is lighter. The United States is pursuing supremacy in space. The president is in Houston to celebrate the life of Representative Albert Thomas as well as the birth of Houston as a critical hub in our space program. In a light and breezy dinner speech, he looks backward twenty-seven years, to 1936, to commemorate the year when Representative Thomas was first elected to Congress. Then he looks forward twenty-seven years—to 1990—and begins to use visionary language about the future of space exploration. Here are his words:

> In 1990, the age of space will be entering its second phase, and our hopes in it to preserve the peace, to make sure that in this great new sea, as on earth, the United States is second to none. And that is why I salute Albert Thomas and those Texans whom you sent to Washington in his time and since then, who recognize the needs and trends today in the sixties so that when we meet here in 1990 they will look back on what we did and say that we made the right and wise decisions. "Your old men shall dream dreams, your young men shall see visions," the Bible tells us, and *where there is no vision, the people perish*" (emphasis added).

President Kennedy would not, of course, make it back to Houston in 1990 to celebrate progress toward the vision he invoked in that speech. The next day—in Dallas—he was assassinated, making these words among his very last.

Sir John Templeton: A Spiritual Vision

Sir John Templeton was a genius investor, a visionary philanthropist, and a pioneer in exploring the big questions of life and the cosmos. His creed: "how little we know, how much to learn." Among his many visionary projects was gathering the wisdom of the ages, the time-tested principles, rules, and insights for enabling each of us to lead a full and rich life. It was his belief that the world operates not only according to scientific laws, but also according to spiritual ones. Spirit is built into the very DNA of life. His book, *Worldwide Laws of Life,* describes two hundred spiritual principles gleaned from world

The responsibility of tolerance lies in those
who have the wider vision.

—GEORGE ELIOT, BRITISH NOVELIST

.....

The bravest are surely those who have the
clearest vision of what is before them, glory
and danger alike, and yet notwithstanding,
go out to meet it.

**—THUCYDIDES,
GREEK HISTORIAN OF ATHENS**

religions, philosophical leaders, and spiritual traditions. Here's a small sampling:

- Thanksgiving leads to having more to give thanks for.
- Beautiful thoughts build a beautiful soul.
- You create your own reality.

For our purposes, however, Sir John lists Proverbs 29:18 as the second in the two hundred guiding principles of life. I do not know if placement early in the order matters, but there it is, right up front.

He takes the proverb in a new direction, releasing it from its collective meaning and placing it squarely in the hands of individual people. Vision becomes an essential tool for leading a happy and fulfilling life. For him, vision is a clear and specific goal that matches our calling in life. We'll talk more about this process in chapter 4.

Visualization Propels a Vision

In his essay on Proverbs 29:18, Sir John holds up Henry Ford as a noteworthy visionary. "Ford pictured in his mind's eye the type of automobile he wanted to build at a price most people could afford. He created a mental blueprint of his dream car long before it was even put to paper. Then he pictured great numbers of people buying and driving it." For Sir John, the critical dynamic of this vision story is the process of visualization. Ford imagined it, saw the steps, and willed it to happen. Vision becomes reality. In the language of one of the other spiritual principles noted above, "You create your own reality."

The Henry Ford story reminds me of another inventor, Thomas Edison. Now there is one out-of-the-box visionary. Wendy Kopp, the founder and inspiration behind the Teacher for America program (which encourages some of our nation's best and brightest to become teachers, and to seek positions in places that desperately need great teachers), has a beautiful way of capturing Edison's vision-making energy. It is actually a good way of thinking about vision-in-general:

> When Thomas Edison invented the light bulb, he didn't start by trying to improve the candle. He decided that he wanted better light and went from there.

What's Needed Now: *Global Vision*

Both Roosevelt and Kennedy articulated visions for America, with the former intent on creating economic security and stability and the latter determined to promote supremacy in space and what we now call national security. Both these visions had urgency as a backdrop and a clear focus on mobilizing American citizens to support the vision.

We live in a time now where a sense of

I see America, not in the setting sun of a black
night of despair ahead of us, I see America
in the crimson light of a rising sun fresh from
the burning, creative hand of God. I see great
days ahead, great days possible to men
and women of will and vision . . .

**—CARL SANDBURG, AMERICAN POET,
NOVELIST, AND BIOGRAPHER**

urgency draws the world together to recognize and act on relatively new perceptions of global crises and global interdependence (for both explaining and solving the crises). We don't have a long, shared, international experience in thinking about vision multinationally. The world is finally coming to terms with the idea that our economic, political, ecological, and communications systems are so organically interconnected that efforts to advance human well-being must encompass and draw on the talents of everyone in the global village.

Millennium Development Goals: A Global Approach

Several efforts to weave the world together in common purpose are underway. The most ambitious one is being spearheaded by the United Nations. In 2002, all 191 UN members agreed unanimously to pursue eight worldwide goals by signing the United Nations Millennium Declaration. The eight Millennium Development Goals (MDFs) actually represent a powerful vision. They are long term and require an unprecedented degree of international planning and cooperation. The goals are bold. A definite sense of urgency underlies them. Every one of us on this planet should know them. Most of us—in fact, I'd guess 99 percent—have no idea what they are. The Millennium Development Goals are these:

Goal 1: Eradicate Extreme Hunger and Poverty

Cut in half, between 1990 and 2015, the proportion of people whose income is less than $1 a day

Achieve full and productive employment for all, including women and young people

Cut in half, between 1990 and 2015, the proportion of people who suffer from hunger

Goal 2: Achieve Universal Primary Education

Ensure that, by 2015, children everywhere—boys and girls alike—will be able to complete a full course of primary schooling

Goal 3: Promote Gender Equality and Empower Women

Eliminate gender disparity in primary and secondary education at all levels of education no later than 2015

Goal 4: Reduce Child Mortality

Reduce by two-thirds, between 1990 and 2015, the mortality rate of children under five years old

Goal 5: Improve Maternal Health

Reduce by three-quarters, between 1990 and 2015, the maternal mortality rate

Nothing happens unless first a dream.

**—CARL SANDBURG, AMERICAN POET,
NOVELIST, AND BIOGRAPHER**

Goal 6: Combat HIV/AIDS, Malaria, and Other Diseases

Cut in half the spread of HIV/AIDS and begin to reverse it by 2015

Achieve, by 2010, universal access to HIV/AIDS treatment for all those who need it

Cut in half and begin to reverse the incidence of malaria by 2015

Goal 7: Ensure Environmental Sustainability

Cut in half by 2015 the proportion of people without sustainable access to safe drinking water and basic sanitation

Goal 8: Develop a Global Partnership for Development

Ensure developed nations support developing nations with trade, aid, and relief of debt.

In partnership with developing countries, develop strategies for youth employment.

Amen. Sign me up. Tell me what I can do.

Vision is one thing. The logic model for how a vision will be achieved is something else entirely. Unfortunately, few of us even know the goals or the players or our personal role, and this constitutes a significant problem.

For the millennium goals, governments are the big players. So how is ours doing? Who can I call to press for action and accountability? And the businesses I buy from—many with international markets—like 3M, General Mills, Cargill, Best Buy, Apple, Sony, Pepsi. Are they pulling their weight? How do I find out? Whom do I call? Because of the lack of importance of these issues in our mainstream media, we rarely pose these questions to leaders in government and at various corporations, and even less often receive answers from them.

Making a Shared Commitment Work

Social change visions require not only big ideas, but inspiring calls to action and practical ways that citizens can connect and contribute. Left to their own devices, governments will usually foul this up. In partnership, we just might get somewhere. I'd be more optimistic if once, just once, a civic organization, a congregation, a newspaper, or a TV station had shared the vision, provided an update on our progress, and given us the opportunity to do something—even if it was to send for a bumper sticker that said something like this: THE MILLENNIUM DEVELOPMENT GOALS ROCK.

Climate change and global warming demand a big vision statement that draws countries, communities, and citizens into a shared commitment. Here's precisely where the vision concepts of long term, big picture, interdependence, and all hands on deck can come together powerfully and dramatically. On this issue, citizens, neighborhoods, and communities can be—and often are—the catalytic vision-makers. As in so many spheres of promoting the social good, vision and action are mobilized as a social movement far in advance of government policy. It took a civil rights movement, for example, to trigger civil rights legislation. It took a suffrage movement to catalyze the right to vote. Vision-at-its-best inspires and mobilizes citizens. For my money, grassroots vision trumps top-down vision every time.

A Cautionary Note: Vision Gone Awry

This is a good place to offer a warning: Vision can be dangerous. History is replete with visions and visionaries that play to the dark side. Calls for racial purity, ethnic cleansing, and "My religion is better than your religion" are among the ideas that too often have been at the center of someone's demonic vision. Charisma can fall into the wrong hands.

The obvious point is that not all visions are created equal. The litmus test for noble social vision is whether its achievement clearly advances the well-being of those who have the least.

A VISION FOR OUR CHILDREN

Kasserian ingera? is a traditional greeting of the Masai people of Kenya and Tanzania. Instead of greeting each other with "How are you?" they utter the greeting, "How are the children?" The traditional response is *sapati ingera* ("All the children are well").

In the United States and many other nations as well, we could not answer that question in the affirmative. The reality is that some of our children are thriving—yet far

It may be that those who do most,

dream most.

**—STEPHEN LEACOCK, CANADIAN WRITER
AND ECONOMIST**

too many are not. In America, the data about child well-being is chilling. Let's start with economics. According to the National Center for Children in Poverty, some 12 million kids live in "poor" families—flat out below the federal poverty line, which is $19,350 for a family of four. Another 28 million live in families that are "low-income," which is defined as having a household income (again, for a family of four) between $19,350 and $38,700. Altogether, nearly 40 percent of children seventeen or younger live in poor or low-income families. Try to buy family vacations, trips to summer camp, music lessons, sports gear, or trips to museums on that, while also covering the basic costs of housing, food, transportation, and medical care.

Then let's look at how our nation is doing in preventing so-called risk behaviors. In studies conducted by Search Institute, we monitor young people's engagement in patterns of health-compromising behaviors like alcohol and tobacco use, violence, attempted suicide, illicit drug use, school absenteeism, and acts of vandalism or theft. Our studies show that about 65 percent of twelve- to eighteen-year-olds report one or more of these risky behavior patterns. By *pattern,* we mean three or more occurrences in a one-year period.

Risk behaviors are developmental signposts focusing on things our society seeks to prevent. Just as important, a society needs to look at how well it is providing the developmental nutrients that are necessary for growing healthy, successful, and responsible young people. These nutrients—or developmental assets as we call them—include essentials like sustained relationships with caring adults; neighborhoods where adults know, protect, listen to, and engage their children; frequent opportunities for young people to serve others; engagement in the creative arts; and boundaries consistently articulated and monitored. Unfortunately, *most* youth in

America receive only a minimal dose of the positive nutrients they need to thrive.

Children Being Left Behind

So, sliced and diced several different ways, a theme emerges. We now know, based on consistent and disconcerting evidence, that many of our nation's children are being left behind. This, of course, ought to be seen as an issue of considerable urgency, right up there with other big social issues. The stewardship of our children's lives is as important as the stewardship of our natural resources. While this wound festers, it certainly does not help that the percentage of the federal budget allocated to supporting our children is in decline. This means that our national investment in schools, social services geared to young people and after-school programs, is being reduced at a time when research studies reveal that we need them more than ever.

At last a vision has been vouchsafed to us of our

life as a whole. We see the bad with the good. . . .

With this vision we approach new affairs.

Our duty is to cleanse, to reconsider, to restore,

to correct the evil without impairing the good,

to purify and humanize every process of our

common life, without weakening

or sentimentalizing it.

—WOODROW WILSON, U.S. PRESIDENT

Now is the time when vision is critical. Its clear articulation is needed to put our nation on alert; draw citizens, communities, and government together in common purpose; and give direction and impetus for concrete action. That's a tall order, of course. I think of two people whose visions are well worth paying attention to—Geoffrey Canada and Marian Wright Edelman.

Two Visionaries for Our Time
Geoffrey Canada: Harlem Children's Zone

Geoffrey Canada is the charismatic leader who created and now guides the Harlem Children's Zone in New York City. Central Harlem is home to far too many young people for whom social institutions—including schools, neighborhoods, and families—are broken. Geoffrey knows that to build successful lives, many changes are needed simultaneously. So, driven by a vision of transforming an entire community, he has helped to redesign schools, engage families, expand social services, and introduce new after-school programs.

The vision is compelling. It requires significant investment. The annual budget for this multiblock initiative serving 7,400 kids a year is over $50 million. Here is a case where big vision is able to attract big philanthropic dollars. The support is rolling in and other cities are exploring how to replicate this bold social experiment.

Marian Wright Edelman:
Children's Defense Fund

There's no one quite like Marian Wright Edelman. For four decades, she has been the premier national champion for a just approach to America's marginalized and dispossessed children. She is the founder and president of the Children's Defense Fund in Washington, D.C., and the author of several inspirational and visionary books. I recommend *The Measure of Our Success: A Letter to My Children and Yours*. Hers is the dominant and sustained voice for reordering our nation's priorities so that children—particularly poor children—are given a fair chance to become whole and hopeful.

Her vision: a nation that ensures that each and every child has enough to eat, quality medical care, access to great schools, and a caring place to call home. (On this last point, think foster care, abandoned children, and children of prisoners, to name a few of the ways too many children become disconnected from caring families early and forever.)

AWAKENING THE SLEEPING GIANT: JOINING HANDS IN COMMON CAUSE

On a parallel track, my professional home, Search Institute, is trying to unite and mobilize towns and cities to awaken the sleeping giant. The sleeping giant is the capacity of citizens and systems to join hands in common cause. Capacity yes; action no. Unfortunately, in most cities, the systems called schools, families, neighborhoods, churches, employers, after-school programs, and city government are isolated and warring turfs. Child development is governed by silos of responsibility with too little sense of interdependence and common purpose. And the citizens in many of our communities have lost sight of their capacity to be on the team for growing great kids.

Not surprisingly, most cities have many programs and services, but no vision that draws them together and inspires action. Vision is a necessary (but not sufficient) element in unleashing the natural but dormant power of a city.

Identifying Universal
"Developmental Assets"

The process we at Search Institute used began with identifying a set of universal building blocks of development (i.e., supports and opportunities that have been shown through research to produce positive outcomes) and, whenever possible, to identify those components that have been shown to work for all kids, across gender, age, race, ethnicity, and family income. We called this the framework of developmental assets. We then took a draft of the framework to parents, educators, and community leaders, and, in a series of guided dialogues, asked for input on our draft and sought advice on other universally acknowledged developmental supports. These conversations were held in urban centers and small towns in all regions of the country. They included exchanges with elders of Native American tribes and

Poetry is not only dream and vision; it is the
skeleton architecture of our lives. It lays the
foundation for a future of change, a bridge across
our fears of what has never been before.

—AUDRE LORDE, AMERICAN AUTHOR

immigrant communities. The goal was to pinpoint developmental elements that all citizens would want for their own children; that is, whenever parents anywhere looked at the list, they would say, "I want my kids to experience these, too."

What emerged in 1995 was the framework of forty developmental assets and a survey instrument that, when administered to all or most middle school and high school youth, provides a portrait of how well a city is doing through the asset lens. More than two thousand cities in the United States, and a growing number in other nations, have commissioned this asset portrait.

The portrait stirs a community's soul. Here are nine of the assets that nearly every city that has done the study discovers fewer than half of their young people possess:

- *Caring adults:* Young person receives support from three or more nonparent adults.

- *Caring neighborhood:* Young person experiences caring neighbors.

- *Caring school:* School (both teachers and peers) provides a caring and encouraging environment.

- *Community values youth:* Young person perceives that adults in the community value youth.

- *Youth as resources:* Young person perceives that adults view youth as positive community resources rather than as problems to be managed.

- *Service to others:* Young person volunteers in the community one hour or more per week.

- *Adult role models:* Parents and other adults model positive, responsible behavior.

- *Creative activities*: Young person spends three or more hours per week in lessons or practice in music, theater, or other arts.

- *Family boundaries:* Family has clear rules and consequences for violating those rules, and monitors the young person's whereabouts.

Creating a Community Vision

When community leaders assemble to discuss their asset report, something crucial happens—actually two things. First, they discover that assigning blame to others misses the point. And that is because the assets require all hands on deck. As I often say, "If you breathe, you are on the team." Second, a consensus begins to build around the possibility of transforming community life to ensure that all young people grow up asset-rich. Here's where the idea of creating a community vision kicks in. With only a bit of help from us, communities begin to frame where they want to be. Across the hundreds of U.S. and Canadian cities that now use the developmental assets as their organizing

The difference between what we do and what
we are capable of doing would suffice to solve
most of the world's problems.

**—MAHATMA GANDHI, INDIAN POLITICAL
AND SPIRITUAL LEADER**

framework for change, there is a beautiful rainbow of vision statements. Among them: "a city where all young people thrive"; "a city where all youth grow up asset-rich"; and "a community that puts children first." Many communities develop vision teams, a cross-sector group of leaders and youth whose job is to keep the vision front and center, and empower the community to pick up the gauntlet and run with it.

What I so often hear when visiting these vision-based community initiatives is the word *hope*. Maybe that word emerges because the asset model invites in a broad spectrum of actors so that people are released from the burden of "having to do it all myself." Or perhaps it is because the language of assets invites the creation of a community vision that finally, after many years of trying, unites groups and sectors that previously focused exclusively on protecting their own turf.

Hope. This is an important part of vision.

I don't know what your destiny will be, but
the one thing I know; the only ones among you
who will really be happy are those who will have
sought and found how to serve.

**—ALBERT SCHWEITZER, ALSATIAN THEOLOGIAN
AND PHYSICIAN**

Hope that the future is bright and that we the people have some control over creating that future. This book began with the words of Arundhati Roy. I hold them up here too to remind us that change is in the air.

Another world is not only possible,
she is on her way.

On a quiet day, I can hear her breathing.

....

Hope is the thing with feathers

That perches in the soul.

And sings the tune

Without the words,

and never stops at all.

—EMILY DICKINSON,
AMERICAN POET

....

4. VISION & THE HUMAN SOUL

....

SOCIAL VISION helps us imagine how to heal a broken world. It challenges us to move beyond the status quo, the conventional, and invites us to take a giant leap forward in re-creating our communities, our nations, and the world.

Spiritual vision addresses a different kind of brokenness. It's much more personal. The symptoms are anxiety, depression, separation, pain, and suffering. Søren Kierkegaard called it our "fear and trembling." This picture of life is sometimes called the "human condition." And it's a condition we all try to circumvent or escape. We'll try anything—excessive busyness, self-medication, professionally prescribed medication, sleep, denial—to avoid facing this reality of life. But the undercurrent is always there. This capacity to undermine our achievements, beat ourselves up, see darkness all around, attribute ill motives to others, mistreat others, be skeptical, worry, and get angry—all of this is always there, knocking at the door. Let your guard down, and you find yourself wallowing in the human condition. You get the picture. I certainly do.

EVERYDAY PERCEPTIONS: A DISTORTION OF REALITY

Is this the way it has to be? Are we missing something? My answers are, in turn, no and yes. I take inspiration from a long line of spiritual visionaries, each of whom is seeking to teach me that everyday reality, as most of us experience it, is a distortion of the true nature of things. Spiritual visionaries, like social visionaries, invite us into a new way of seeing and being. In this chapter, I'll point out some who speak to me and delve into several of the common threads that tie their visions together. I will also recommend a handful of books that have illuminated my path.

Buddha and Jesus are the prime exemplars of spiritual vision, particularly if we measure this concept by impact and sustainability. We're talking here about a long-term impact of 2,500 years on the one hand and 2,000 on the other. Each now has hundreds of millions of followers, with most being adherents of an organized religion that neither Buddha nor Jesus aspired to start. As Marcus Borg tells us in *Jesus and Buddha: The Parallel Sayings*, their real aim was to encourage a "perceptual shift" in how we know and experience ourselves and each other. How we see life and the nature of reality is distorted. Buddha

If we had a keen vision and feeling of all ordinary
human life, it would be like hearing the grass grow
and the squirrel's heart beat, and we should die of
that roar which lies on the other side of silence.
As it is, the best of us walk about well
wadded with stupidity.

—GEORGE ELIOT, BRITISH NOVELIST

. . . . .

Dreams come true; without that possibility,
nature would not incite us to have them.

—JOHN UPDIKE, AMERICAN NOVELIST

and Jesus illuminate the hidden truth. Buddha became known as "the enlightened one," and Jesus' vision, as Borg describes it, is captured in the well-known verse from "Amazing Grace": "I was blind, but now I see."

To what are we blind? What is the hidden truth? Now it really gets interesting. Powerful answers to these questions come from some extraordinary visionaries. For both Buddha and Jesus, blindness comes from ego or, more specifically, the focus on self as the operating principle of life. Self separates us from others; it is transient, illusory. It is the primary source of suffering according to Buddha, and the primary source of sin for Jesus. Look at the symmetry of these two sacred sayings: "Those who want to save their life will lose it" and "With the relinquishing of all thought and egotism, the enlightened one is liberated." Guess who said which.

Self or ego blinds us to spirit, the source of generosity and understanding and wisdom, and the glue that binds us to all of life. In *Living Buddha, Living Christ*, Thich Nhat Hanh, the exiled Vietnamese Buddhist master, tells us spirit is the animator of life and the connective tissue. "When we are in touch with the highest spirit in ourselves we too are a Buddha, filled with the Holy Spirit, and we become very tolerant, very open, very deep, and very understanding."

THE TRANSFORMATIVE POWER OF SPIRIT & VISION

Spirit animates and spirit connects. Let's delve a bit more deeply into these two active verbs. As we do so, the tie between spirit and vision will become clear.

William James, the noted Harvard psychologist and philosopher, published *The Varieties of Religious Experience* in 1902. The book is not really about religion. It is about spirit, that "unseen reality" identified across time by visionaries of the soul. James digs deeply into worldwide sacred texts, the writings of mystics, the poetry of the Transcendentalists, and the science and philosophy of human consciousness, which, incidentally, was as big a deal a hundred years ago as it is now. Here's one point about this long-term search for "unseen reality": In 1897, philosopher Ralph Waldo Trine published a book called *In Tune with the Infinite*. It sold 1.5 million copies.

One of James's conclusions is that people who are in touch with spirit are utterly transformed. They live in a "state of assurance" that confers "the loss of all worry, the sense that all is well with one, the peace, the harmony, the *willingness* to be, even though the outer conditions should remain the same." Everything looks new and different. "An appearance of newness beautifies every object." As theologian Jonathan Edwards put it, "Before, I used to be uncommonly terrified

It is where life is fundamental and free that men
develop the vision needed to reveal the human
soul in the blossoms it puts forth.

—FRANK LLOYD WRIGHT, AMERICAN ARCHITECT

. . . . .

A baby is God's opinion that life should go on.

**—CARL SANDBURG, AMERICAN POET,
NOVELIST, AND BIOGRAPHER**

. . . . .

Dreams are illustrations . . . from the book your
soul is writing about you.

**—MARSHA NORMAN,
AMERICAN PLAYWRIGHT**

with thunder and to be struck with terror when I saw a thunderstorm rising; but now, on the contrary, it rejoices me."

How Spirit
Animates & Connects Us All

Talk about perpetual shift. The state of spirit illuminates and animates a life. Clouds lift. Nothing looks the same. As Walt Whitman said in the preface to his *Leaves of Grass*, "Re-examine all you have been told at school or church or in any book, dismiss whatever insults your own soul."

And spirit connects. If there's one major theme that runs through the spiritual transformation literature, it concerns the unity of life, the intersection and oneness of life. Living in the modern world—and in a society that's organized around "me" as opposed to "we"—it is almost impossible to know and experience unity. Unity, though, is the bedrock insight of spiritual visionaries. Spirit is, as theologian Matthew Fox put it, the Great River. All of life is embedded, linked, connected, one. I think this is what St. Paul meant when he wrote: "It is in God that we live, and move, and have our being" (Acts 17:28).

Walt Whitman is the poet of unity. He has spoken to countless generations of seekers. These words speak to me:

> And I know that the hand of God is
> the elderhand of my own,
>
> And I know that the spirit of God is
> the eldest brother of my own,
>
> And that all the men ever born are also
> my brothers . . . and the women my
> sisters and lovers,
>
> And that a keelson of the creation
> is love;

And limitless are leaves stiff or
drooping in the fields,

And brown ants in the little wells
beneath them,

And mossy scabs of the wormfence,
and heaped stones, and elder and
mullen and pokeweed.

LOVE: THE UNIFYING FORCE
IN THE UNIVERSE

Every time I read James's *Varieties*, I find one
section and one quote that stops me in my
tracks. It is the ultimate spiritual vision. It
elucidates the abstract concept of unity while
at the same time capturing the idea that the
unseen energy force is love. The section is in
the chapter on mysticism. It is here that James
draws on the experience of Dr. R. M. Bucke,
a Canadian psychiatrist, who published a

Hope, like the gleaming taper's light,

Adorns and cheers our way;

And still, as darker grows the night,

Emits a brighter ray.

**—OLIVER GOLDSMITH,
BRITISH-IRISH AUTHOR**

.....

Young people have an almost biological

destiny to be hopeful.

**—MARSHALL GANZ, AMERICAN LABOR
ORGANIZER AND LECTURER**

remarkable book in 1901 called *Cosmic Consciousness*. Here is Bucke's account:

I had spent the evening in a great city, with two friends, reading and discussing poetry and philosophy. We parted at midnight. I had a long drive in a hansom to my lodging. My mind, deeply under the influence of the ideas, images, and emotions called up by the reading and talk, was calm and peaceful. I was in a state of quiet, almost passive enjoyment, not actually thinking, but letting ideas, images, and emotions flow of themselves, as it were, through my mind. All at once, without warning of any kind, I found myself wrapped in a flame-colored cloud. For an instant I thought of fire, an immense conflagration somewhere close by in that great city; the next, I knew that the fire was within myself. Directly afterward there came upon me a sense of exultation, of immense joyousness accompanied or immediately followed by an intellectual illumination impossible to describe. Among other things, I did not merely come to believe, but I saw that the universe is not composed of dead matter, but is, on the contrary, a living Presence; I became conscious in myself of eternal life. It was not a conviction that I would have eternal life, but a consciousness that I possessed eternal life then; I saw that all men are immortal; that the cosmic order is such that without any peradventure all things work together for the good of each and all; that the foundation principle of the world, of all the worlds, is what we call love, and that the happiness of each and all is in the long run absolutely certain. The vision lasted a few seconds and was gone; but the memory of it and the sense of the reality of what it taught has remained during the quarter of a century which has since elapsed. I knew that what the vision showed was true. I had attained to a point of view from which I saw that it must be true. That view, that conviction, I may say that consciousness, has never, even during periods of the deepest depression, been lost.

The Plains Indians probably don't use the phrase *cosmic consciousness* to capture their historic wisdom about vision and the quest to discover it, but they sure know how to access it. The ritual of vision quest begins with severance from the noise and clutter of everyday life. (In traditional Lakota culture, the term that we translate as *vision quest* literally means "crying for a vision.") This can take days of self-denial and isolation. As the body and mind are cleansed, the person becomes reconnected to spirit, to source. When vision

Reach high, for the stars lie hidden in your soul.

Dream deep, for every dream precedes the goal.

—PAMELA VAULL STARR, AMERICAN POET,

ARTIST, AND WRITER

.....

Your vision will become clear only when you

can look into your own heart....

Who looks outside, dreams;

who looks inside, awakes.

—CARL JUNG, SWISS PSYCHIATRIST

AND PSYCHOANALYST

emerges, the visionary has an obligation to return to his community and live out the vision.

COMPASSION:
THE TRUE NATURE OF REALITY

This process of illumination is triggered in many ways, of course, and it sources and fuels some of the most compelling social visions of our time. Both Desmond Tutu, the former archbishop of Cape Town, South Africa, and His Holiness the Dalai Lama continue to articulate compelling and urgent visions of the possible. Both are recipients of the Nobel Peace Prize. And both show how spirit animates, connects, and challenges us. The true nature of reality is compassion, they remind us.

Tutu, in *God Has a Dream: A Vision of Hope for Our Time*, says: "All over this magnificent world God calls us to extend His Kingdom

But history will judge you, and as the years pass,
you will ultimately judge yourself, in the extent to
which you have used your gifts and talents
to lighten and enrich the lives of your fellow men.
In your hands lies the future of your world
and the fulfillment of the best qualities
of your own spirit.

—ROBERT F. KENNEDY, U.S. SENATOR
AND ATTORNEY GENERAL

of shalom—peace and wholeness—of justice, goodness, of compassion, of caring, of sharing, of laughter, of joy, and of reconciliation." And the Dalai Lama, in *Ancient Wisdom, Modern World—Ethics for a New Millennium,* tells us that compassion "is the source of all lasting happiness and joy." It is the method by which all noble social change happens. Peace. Justice. Reconciliation. It's a matter of love.

Love. It's the nature of things.

....

A child's world is fresh and new and beautiful,

full of wonder and excitement. It is our misfortune

that for most of us that clear-eyed vision, that

true instinct for what is beautiful and awe-

inspiring, is dimmed and even lost

before we reach adulthood.

—RACHEL CARSON,
AMERICAN ENVIRONMENTAL ACTIVIST

....

5. CREATING ONE'S PERSONAL VISION

....

VISION is the breakthrough perception of possibility—for the world, our society, our communities, and ourselves. You do not have to be Albert Schweitzer or His Holiness the Dalai Lama to create a vision. Vision-making is a human capacity open to all of us. Each of us has it. Sometimes we just need a nudge. So think of this concluding chapter as that nudge.

WRITE A VISION STATEMENT

Think of something bigger than you and your own ambitions. Vision isn't about your personal success or achievements. Vision's primary referent should be something that makes the world better. It should also dovetail with something for which you have deep passion and a sense that you can make a contribution to its actualization.

I find a good way to do this is to complete the following sentence:

*I imagine a world [or nation, or community]
where* _____*.*

You should fill in this sentence three or four ways, put them on your computer, desk, refrigerator, or nightstand, and contemplate—quietly and thoughtfully—the one that really speaks to you.

When I do this, I can easily generate candidates for my vision statement. Some of my possibilities are:

- I imagine a world that falls in love with reading.

- I imagine a world without poverty.

- I imagine a nation with public schools that are great for all kids.

- I imagine a nation where any kid who wants to can learn to play tennis.

- I imagine a world where the development of a voice-activated software system will convert the spoken word into text while making no mistakes.

- I imagine a city that welcomes immigrants and sees them as resources.

- I imagine a world where conflict is resolved peacefully.

- I imagine a nation that makes its children its top priority.

Practice means to perform, over and over again in the face of all obstacles, some act of vision, of faith, of desire. Practice is a means of inviting the perfection desired.

—MARTHA GRAHAM, AMERICAN MODERN DANCE PIONEER

. . . . .

I touch the future. I teach.

—CHRISTA MCAULIFFE, AMERICAN SCHOOLTEACHER WHO PERISHED IN THE CHALLENGER EXPLOSION

. . . . .

Keep true to the dreams of thy youth.

—FRIEDRICH VON SCHILLER, GERMAN DRAMATIST AND POET

I support anyone or any organization that works toward these visions. I rally, however, around the last one. That's my passion. My capacities are aligned with it.

Once you've written a handful of vision statements you care about, try to align your passion and capacity with the one where you can or are making a contribution. Don't ignore the other ones on your list. Taken together, they provide an extraordinary portal into your soul and the things you stand for.

Use this "I imagine" exercise with your friends, spouse, partner, and children. It provides a wonderful way to know and affirm each other.

KEEP YOUR VISION STATEMENT VISIBLE

When you are comfortable with a vision statement, don't lose sight of it. Make it a computer pop-up or write it on something that you will easily see when life gets busy and hectic. Let it remind you what your life is about and for. Make a habit, every now and then, to contemplate your vision statement and ask the universe for guidance on how you can address it.

REJOICE IN SMALL CONTRIBUTIONS TO YOUR VISION

For most of us, the vision is too big to reach by ourselves or even in our lifetime. I remember visiting the Crazy Horse monument near Rapid City, South Dakota about ten years ago. This carved-in-stone portrait will ultimately be larger and even more majestic than the Black Hills National Monument. The sculpting began decades ago. The original visionary's work has been taken up by his family. When I asked family members how long it would take to finish, they replied, "Another thirty or forty years," and "Long after some of us are gone." They thrive on contributing to a vision that adds to the beauty of the world, even if they may never see the end point.

Celebrate Interdependence

I think part of the compelling nature of vision is that it links us to a community of actors who treasure the same dream. It is good enough to be a bit player in a vision play. We do not need to be the lead actor or actress. We do need, though, to contribute and to see how our role joins with others' in creating a story that enriches the world. As leadership expert Margaret Wheatley put it, "Community is the unit of change." The only way we make progress is together.

Vision enlarges our lives. Vision connects us.

An artist is a dreamer consenting to dream

of the actual world.

**—GEORGE SANTAYANA, SPANISH PHILOSOPHER,
ESSAYIST, POET, AND NOVELIST**

.....

Go confidently in the direction of your dreams!

Live the life you've imagined. As you simplify your

life, the laws of the universe will be simpler.

**—HENRY DAVID THOREAU, AMERICAN PHILOSOPHER,
POET, AND ESSAYIST**

Honor Obligation

Obligation seems like a heavy-duty concept to conclude with. Yes, obligation has some weight to it. In the case of vision, though, the weight is manageable. That's because vision is one of life's best gifts. To dream what is possible and to put oneself in service of that dream is the formula for a life well lived. When we get to the place where we know how our talents and skills can serve a noble purpose, then we must take action. We are obliged. So be it.

Whatever you can do, or dream you can, begin it.

Boldness has genius, power and magic in it.

—JOHANN WOLFGANG VON GOETHE

.....

The least movement is of importance to all nature.

The entire ocean is affected by a pebble.

**—BLAISE PASCAL, FRENCH SCIENTIST, MATHEMATICIAN,
AND RELIGIOUS PHILOSOPHER**

FURTHER READING

....

Benson, Peter L. (2006). *All Kids Are Our Kids: What Communities Must Do to Raise Caring and Responsible Children and Adolescents.* San Francisco: Jossey-Bass.

Bstan-'dzin-rgya-mtsho, Dalai Lama XIV (1999). *Ancient Wisdom, Modern World—Ethics for the New Millennium.* New York: Riverhead Press.

Edelman, Marian Wright (1992). *The Measure of Our Success: A Letter to My Children and Yours.* Boston: Beacon Press.

James, William (1902). *The Varieties of Religious Experience.* Cambridge, MA: Harvard University Press.

Kumar, Satish, and Whitefield, Freddie (Eds.). (2007). *Visionaries: The 20th Century's 100 Most Important Inspirational Leaders*. White River Junction, VT: Chelsea Green Publishing.

Loeb, Paul Rogat (2004). *The Impossible Will Take a Little While: A Citizens' Guide to Hope in a Time of Fear*. New York: Basic Books.

Nhat Hanh, Thich (1995). *Living Buddha, Living Christ*. New York: Riverhead Press.

Tutu, Desmond (2004). *God Has a Dream: A Vision of Hope for Our Time*. New York: Doubleday.